TO: Chad

Bring You Much
Inspiration & Insight.

I Bx

Treasury of a

Man's Thoughts

A Man's Thoughts

On Love, Marriage, and Family

John Momplaisir

John Momplaisir

John Momplaisir

John Momplaisir

Dedications

This Book is Dedicated to My Daughter's

Anecia Momplaisir, Heaven Momplaisir, and

To My Future Wife, Mrs. Momplaisir

Table of Contents

Introduction

Ever since I could remember, I've always desired what our generation refers to as "that old school type of love." This is the type of love where folks fought for each other, and not against each other. This is the kind of love where a man pursued and a woman couldn't resist. During those times, love and romance were highly valued.

This was a time when it took forever to get on the Internet. The beeping and screeching sounds were some of the things we dealt with before getting online. We

waited minutes for our dial-up connections

to boot up. Once that was done, it took

forever to surf because of how slow the

internet was. It was the time when

an American Senator and Republican

Presidential candidate, Bob Dole, endorsed

a drug for erectile dysfunction. This was the

time when so many of us dropped

everything to watch the final moments of

the OJ Simpson trial, even though it aired

in the middle of a work day. It is said that a

record was set for the number of pizzas

ordered that day. We witnessed President

Bill Clinton's ratings for approval go up during the Monica Lewinsky scandal. It was the highest during his whole presidency. This was the time that many predicted the end of the world. The Government predicted a massive technical glitch that could destroy our computers the moment the clock struck midnight on January 1, 2000. There was a huge Y2K scare.

In spite of all that, what stuck with me most about life in the 90's were the music and films. I wasn't a singer or a film critic however, I found the music and movies to be very inspiring. Love, marriage,

and building a family were highly

promoted. I couldn't wait to experience this

love that everyone sang about. My mother

and father instilled family values into my

brothers and I, so desiring a family was

always number one on my list. My

mother loved to tell us stories. Her favorites

were of her and my father and how dad

was the only man that she had ever been

with.

She would tell us of how God had honored the desires of her heart concerning love. As I grew up, I would whisper to myself "It's my turn now" and "I want this love stuff and I want it now."

Love is supposed to be friendship that has caught fire. Love is more than saying "I love you" every night, it also seeks to prove it every day." Love is the glue that sticks two souls together.

Chapter One

I Fell In Love with the Idea of Love

My parents were in transition and in search of a new church home. They knew of my passion for the Bible, so they sent me to a church where most of the youth there were very spiritual. They did this in hopes that it would satisfy my hunger of learning more about God and the Bible.

While I was very serious about my spirituality, I still wanted to be in love.

I eventually met a young lady and thought I was in love. The way her beauty captivated me, I thought "Oh this must be love." I never really cared for dating; I just wanted to find "the one," get married, and go on with my life. She was my first real girlfriend and later became my wife. "This had to be love" I said to myself, because it consumed me. Nothing else mattered. Many warned me of issues that they could see happening in the future, but I didn't care because I thought I was in love. I didn't want to sleep at night. I wanted only to talk to her over the phone until one of us, or the both of us fell asleep. The feeling was ecstasy. It was euphoric and was like Heaven on earth.

I became obsessed with pleasing her. I wanted to know everything about her. "What do you like?" "What do you enjoy?" "What is your favorite restaurant?" "What makes you smile?" I just wanted to make her happy. Her pain became my pain, and it killed me to see her unhappy. Whenever she was unhappy, I would ask myself "What did I do wrong?" "What can I do to fix it?" These questions plagued my mind

whenever she seemed unhappy. My belief

was when you're "in love" with someone,

you'll change your whole life to

accommodate theirs.

It would take some years before I could

realize that this was not love, but rather the

idea of love that I was drawn to. This

relationship became toxic and destructive

for the both of us. I would say to myself, "I

thought love was suppose build you up, not

diminish you." I wanted out, but how do you

leave when you're so public and everyone

around you is looking to you to model what love is supposed to look like for them?

I began to say to myself, "Well, I'll just ride this out" since by this time we had two gorgeous daughters that I was to protect and provide for. It was also my responsibility to model what a man looks like for them. I would whisper to myself, "I have to stay here for them" because they deserve to have their father and mother under the same roof. The family unit is under attack in our generation, and I was determined to keep mine together.

I quickly learned that my decision to stay and remain emotionally attached to toxicity would not only kill me, but also damage my children psychologically and emotionally. I knew after numerous counseling sessions that this was not good for either of us. But, for someone who was bound by others opinions of me, it would take death to get me out.

Chapter Two

The Slow Death

Nothing is worse than being with someone and yet feeling as though you are by yourself. In Genesis 2:18 (NIV), The LORD God said, "It is not good for the man to be alone..." I've always questioned, "Well how is Adam alone being that God is with him?" "Furthermore, Adam had plenty of pets to keep him company," I would think to myself.

I later learned that God interacts with man on a spiritual level, because God is above man and the animals were beneath Him. Adam needed someone that he could connect with on *his* level. See, it is very possible to be in a room full of people and yet, feel alone. Even worse, it is possible to be in a relationship with someone and feel very much alone because they don't get you.

When it becomes difficult to connect with those that we want to connect to, it is human nature to attempt to use force to make it happen.

Force is defined as strength, effort, might, energy, and power. When something doesn't work, we attempt to apply more strength, more effort, and or more energy into it. But sometimes, forcing what doesn't fit can create more of an issue. Forcing what doesn't fit is one way to experience unbearable pain.

Years ago, I wanted a pair of shoes so badly that I purchased the shoes a size smaller because that's all they had available. I convinced myself that it was not that bad. Needless to say, after walking a day in those shoes I realized that I was inflicting pain on myself to look good. I had managed to force a pair of shoes on my feet that did not fit. Everyone thought I was walking with a new swag. They thought that I had adopted a new style of walking, but I knew I was hurting myself. I learned a lesson that day. If I had only applied this lesson to my pursuit of love, my relationship would have been more fulfilling. I learned that day some things can look good and still not be good for you.

Everything That Looks Good Is Not Good For You

Someone once said to me that "the same people who are candy to our eyes can be poisonous to our hearts." They went on to say that "the ingredients and what they possess on the inside must be known, before feeding them to your soul." Everything that looks good is not good for you and everyone who looks good is not necessarily good for you.

While still holding on to what I now know was an emotional attachment and not love, I kept thinking "I am literally dying on the inside" while looking good on the outside.

God can change it right? That was my theological position at the time.

It was then that I was about to learn that not even God is going to force someone to change who doesn't want to change. People like me....when we fall, we fall deep. It was going to take death (in my opinion), to thrust me out of toxicity and into my destiny.

Chapter Three

The Day I Died

Many have reported that it is easier to get over the death of a loved one than to go through a divorce. I often thought that when a relationship or marriage came to an end that each party went their separate ways, and within a day or two just moved on as though it never happened. I would quickly learn that the pain of a broken heart is probably one of the most hurtful experiences that one could ever go through.

There is no other way to explain it. When my heart was broken, I felt like *I died*. It is a known fact that your physical heart is what pumps blood to your body. Leviticus 17: 11(NLT) says, "For the life of the body is in its blood..." It is safe to say that the heart is what pumps the life force of the body. Just like your physical heart is responsible for pumping the life force of your body, your emotional heart is what pumps the life force to your soul. When your physical heart stops beating, one can conclude that life has left the body. When your emotional heart is broken, it feels as though life has stopped flowing to your soul.

Anyone who has ever experienced a broken heart can tell you that although they were still existing, they had stopped living. Not only that, many have literally died from a broken heart. The heart strings in your physical heart can sometimes break after deep emotional trauma. It is known in the medical world that extreme emotional pain can cause the heart to lose its form, and as a result the heart becomes unable to pump blood effectively.

Most people who experience this think they may be having a heart attack and are often misdiagnosed. They are often misdiagnosed because heart attacks are more commonly assumed in medical emergencies. Whether physically or emotionally to experience a broken heart is to experience death. The language of the Bible often refers to a broken heart as a crushed spirit. In Proverbs 18:14(NIV) a broken heart or a crushed spirit is compared to sickness. "The human spirit can endure in sickness, but a crushed spirit who can bear?" The Biblical text poses the rhetorical question of who can bear a broken heart because the feeling is truly almost unbearable. In Proverbs 17:22(NIV) it says, "A cheerful heart is good medicine, but A CRUSHED SPIRIT DRIES UP THE BONES."

Medical professionals have made it clear that for your bone marrow to dry up is an indication that blood or the life force of the body is not flowing. When your blood flow is affected, it could be because the heart has been broken, and this prevents life from flowing. In the same manner, when the life force of your soul is not flowing it feels as though your love life has dried up

and died. Allow me to stop and prophesy to

all who have suffered from a broken heart,

although your bones may have dried up

God will cause life to flow as it happened in

the valley of dry bones with the Prophet

Ezekiel... (See Ezekiel 37:9.)

This issue of a broken heart is so serious

that Jesus had a ministry department

devoted solely to the broken-hearted. "The

Spirit of the Lord is upon me, because He

hath anointed me to preach the gospel to

the poor; HE HATH SENT ME TO HEAL

THE BROKENHEARTED, to preach

deliverance to the captives, and recovering

of sight to the blind, to set at liberty them

that are bruised" Luke 4:18 (KJV). I made it

out, because I learned even in the valley of

the shadow of death, (broken heart) God is

always with me.

When I experienced what it was like to

have a broken heart, I experienced what I

called *death*. It was only after I *died* that I

finally heard God speak to me on this

matter. I call it my personal near death

experience. With tears streaming down my

cheeks, I didn't hear an audible voice as I

expressed my anger and grief to God. It

was from within me that I heard Him

whisper "I'm here." See, I felt like God was

as far away from me as He could possibly

be. I thought that there's no way that God

could still be present while I was

experiencing this.

The Lord later directed me to Psalms

34:18(NIV) "The Lord is close to the

brokenhearted and saves those who are

crushed in spirit." I don't care how badly

your heart was broken, I'm telling you that

God is right there and closer than you think.

God reminded me that He never ends

things on a negative note. Even when life

has left us to die, *God is still resurrecting the dead.*

Now that I knew I would not only exist but live again, I had some questions that still needed to be answered. "How could love fail me like this?"

Chapter Four

Doing Our Part

The dead man came out, his hands and
feet wrapped with strips of linen and a cloth
around his face. Jesus said to them, "Take
off the grave clothes and let him go." John
11:14(NIV)

The Bible speaks of a man by the name
of Lazarus. Lazarus is most remembered
as the man whom Jesus raised from the
dead. While reading of what happened to

Lazarus, I noticed something that fascinated me. Jesus raised him from the dead yet even after being resurrected there was still more work that needed to be done. Lazarus, though resurrected was still bound. Even after God delivered Lazarus from the grave, Lazarus still had some attachments from his past that kept him bound. His hands and feet were still tied preventing him from progressing and working towards something better. The fact of the matter is this: the resurrection part is on God, but to be *released* requires your participation. That part is on you.

I learned that it is my duty not to keep going back to whatever or whoever had me bound me in the first place. Whether it is through emotional connection or through the mental torment of unanswered questions, release yourself and move on. It is your duty to remain free. When God resurrects you from something or someone that killed you emotionally, it is your responsibility to forgive. Free yourself from anything that attaches itself to you in efforts to keep you bound. "Well John, how could they hurt me and move on so quickly?" The answer is, if you think everyone has the same kind of heart that you have, then you will keep finding yourself going right back to what killed you and had you bound in the first place.

You will have to learn to forgive, even without an apology. You will have to learn to be free, even if they see nothing wrong with their behavior. One of the greatest lessons that life taught me was you can never change an individual who sees nothing wrong with how they've hurt you. It is up to you to do your part, stay free, and live. I was once in a place where I thought I needed those who hurt me to help me heal.

John Momplaisir

They taught me that it is my responsibility

to do my part to be free and to stay free.

Chapter Five

Love Never Fails

"LOVE NEVER FAILS. But where there are prophecies, they will cease; where there are tongues, they will be stilled; where there is knowledge, it will pass away" 1 Corinthians 13:8(NIV).

The Bible said, "Love never fails." I began to ponder and repeat this to myself that love never fails. So what if it fails?

"Surely, there has to be at least one case of love failing" I said to myself. After deep thought and consideration, I was at peace with this text. I concluded that if it fails it was never love to begin with because love never fails. This love stuff plagued my mind again. What is this love stuff all about? If it isn't that feeling I get when I hear some 90's R&B music, then what is it? If it's not that feeling that comes over me after watching the films "The Woods" and "Love & Basketball," then what is this love stuff?

The Bible has a whole chapter on it and yet most of us are either recovering from what we thought was love or daydreaming about finding love. I couldn't leave this alone, because people like me aren't normal and don't want normal love. If I'm going to love, I want to love someone to the highest capacity possible. I now believe that love must first be received in order to be given. I know that God is not only the giver of love, but God *is* love. (See 1 John 4:8.) How can you give something you do not have? I learned that I had to receive God's love in order to love another to the capacity that I desire, and that love always hopes. This love is not found in a particular relationship, it's found in God. Since God is love and God never fails, then real love never fails.

Love is patient

Love is kind

Chapter Six

Love Always Hopes

Right in the middle of me attempting to learn more about love, I asked myself after tasting *death* (a heart break) "Why do you even want to love?" Memories of all that I had gone through within the twelve years of what I call hell on earth revisited me. In spite of it all, including the possibility of going through it all over again and quenching the life force of my own soul; I just couldn't give up on love.

Many have advised me that this time I may not be so fortunate physically, as they asked me what is wrong with me. "I love too hard", someone said. Another said "You feel things on a level that's not normal, it's not that deep." One friend described me as a hopeless romantic who won't stop, until I die. I corrected her and said there's nothing hopeless about love, and I would prefer to be called a hopeful romantic. As long as there is life in me, I will forever have hope. A popular portion of scripture says, "Love is patient, love is kind. It does not envy, it does not boast, it is not proud. It does not dishonor others, it is not self-seeking, it is not easily angered, it keeps no record of wrongs. Love does not delight in evil, but rejoices with the truth. It always protects, always trusts, ALWAYS HOPES, always perseveres."(1 Corinthians 13:4-7)

Love resides on the inside of me and because of that I cannot give up. No heartbreak, failed marriage, disappointments and or betrayals could ever stop the hope of me loving someone; because love always hopes.

Chapter Seven

Commitment

All I want is for someone to choose me and to keep choosing me.

While learning about love and relationships, I pondered on whether or not love is the only thing needed to make any relationship work. There's always the issue of what if another comes along, then what? Is it possible for someone to desire to find someone better to love? Absolutely. Truth be told, no matter how handsome/beautiful, intelligent, funny, well-dressed, charming or gifted you may be, there will always be another that your significant other may perceive to be better. In addition to love, one must understand commitment.

Commitment says no matter what else presents itself or how well packaged it is, I'm in a covenant. It says I would not risk losing what we have for the possibility of something else. It is commitment that secures a relationship not love. It is very possible to love someone and not be committed to them. I want someone to love me with mutual passion and intensity, but even more than that I want someone who is equally committed. Commitment says not only do I choose you, but I will keep choosing you. It says a few moments of pleasure is not worth sacrificing what we've built. Commitment makes an individual wake up with the decision already made every day to love you, whether they feel like it or not. I was always drawn to the stories of those who remained happily married after 30 years, 40 years and in one case an older couple I read about was married for 65 years. When reading about them I would say, "I want that "grow old together" type of love." When these couples were asked, "What's the secret to remaining married for so long?" They all responded: "commitment." Some said they fell in and out of love many times, but they were committed to being married to that individual. So to me that means love me, but be committed to being with me and only me.

Chapter Eight

Where Are We Going?

Never marry an individual who is not aligned to your purpose or is in conflict with your destiny. While love will always be the glue that attaches two individuals together and commitment will be what keeps that glue from ever wearing out, there is still one more important factor. That factor is whether or not we are compatible. I can be in love and yet never have a successful relationship or marriage. Why? Because everyone isn't headed in the same direction. I made up in my mind not just to marry because of love, but I want purpose attached to all that love. I learned that if I'm going to spend the rest of my life with someone, the person must complement my anointing and not be in conflict with my destiny. Some people love one another but struggle because not only are they not on the same page. Some aren't even reading the same book.

My prayers have now shifted because my experiences have taught me that when someone does not understand your purpose, they'll compete with what you were born to do, and they will destroy you in the name of love. It sounds like this: "Do you have to be preacher?" "Give up preaching and just love on me." "Why pursue your dreams? Let's just focus on us." This is what we know as being "unequally yoked." When the Apostle Paul addressed being equally yoked, it appears that he spoke to the obvious issues that may arise as it pertains to beliefs. The principle of being equally yoked is much more profound than what it appears to be at the surface level. A yoke is a wooden bar that connects two oxen to each other and to the burden they're assigned to carry. The two oxens had to match. They had to be compatible. If the balance was way off, it would cause one to do all of the carrying while the other puts no effort in. An "unequally yoked" couple causes the load to go around in circles.

When oxen are unequally yoked, they cannot perform the task set before them. Instead of working together, they're at odds with one another. There is a component to being equally yoked that deals with sharing the task set before us. So the question becomes are we effective as a pair or destructive? If we're not going forward, then where are we going? Everyone is not a good fit for you and you can't just take anyone with you where you are going.

I WANT A

MARRIAGE MORE
Beautiful Than
OUR WEDDING

Chapter Nine

Prepare For What You Pray For

All I want is a marriage more beautiful than our wedding.

One of the biggest decision you will ever make is who you want to share your life with. If marriage is that important, why do we not invest more into it? I'm not talking about the wedding. I'm talking about the *marriage*. While I absolutely love weddings, we invest all this money into an event that's supposed to last a few hours and invest very little into the marriage which is supposed to last a lifetime. It is known that anything you invest your time, money, and energy into becomes more important to you. So, if I invest my time, money, and energy into having a great marriage it makes sense that the return on my marriage would be even better than that of my wedding.

Personally, I want a marriage more beautiful than my wedding so I'm going to work towards that. Why wait until I get married to be a man worth marrying? As a man of God, I will remain faithful to my wife even if I don't have one yet, because anything I pray for I should prepare for. I don't ever want to be one who desires marriage, but yet refuses to give up my single ways in order to get married. If I'm going to have marriage goals, then I need to put in the effort that reflects a person who is ready for marriage.

I am of the belief that the best time to prepare for your marriage is before you are married. So in addition to preparing for our wedding, we will also invest and prepare for our marriage. Pre-marital counseling will be a must for us. I refuse to wait for something to go wrong and then seek counselors to aid in repairing it. We will also find an older couple who can mentor us throughout our marriage and serve as a couple we can be accountable to. I believe it's your level of preparation that makes for marriage material. Proverb 18:22 says "He who finds a wife, finds a good thing and have obtained favor from the Lord (KJV).

It appears to me that when this man finds her, she's already a wife. She's a wife not because she's married, but because

she's wife material. If that be true

concerning the wife, then it only makes

sense to me that this man who finds this

wife is already husband material. What

does this mean? It means I have a lot of

work to do in order to become that man

worth marrying. While I desire marriage

badly, I mean I really, really, really want

it...like y'all don't understand how much I

want it, I know the difference between

desire and being ready. Someone once

said, "If a man expects a woman to be an

angel, then he must create a heaven for

her to live in" and I am of the belief that a man should be able to cover his wife spiritually, emotionally and financially. I'm not rushing, because you don't have to rush anything that will last a lifetime.

I am in a season of preparation and my prayer is for God to make me into a man worth marrying. The Lord is not finished with me yet. I'm still petty and deliverance is a process. I believe in love. I still believe in Godly marriages.

I believe in forever; and I also know that

John Jeffrey Momplaisir is still being

customized by God to be that man worth

marrying for his future wife, whoever she is.

Chapter Ten

The Ephesians 5 Man: The Man Worth Marrying

Most women have tons of women who teach them and model for them what it is to be a wife. In fact, many women were practicing for marriage at a very early age. They practiced by pairing baby dolls together, reading romance novels, and hearing other women share their love stories with them.

For men, this means we are years behind them and must play catch up. Even when most women get older, they often refer to a passage in the Bible to mirror the type of wife they want to be. You always hear many women talking about the virtuous woman and how she's this and how she's that. Oh, the Proverbs 31 woman is a woman who does this and that. They write books, teach, and even hold empowerment seminars on this very topic. Where's the Proverbs 32 Man? Wait, he doesn't exist. Why? Because the book of Proverbs only has 31 Chapters.

Women already have the upper hand on being married because they've been practicing and they have the Proverbs 31 woman to help them. They tell us very little about the virtuous woman's husband. Yeah, he calls her blessed and praises her, but is that it? In my search for what it means to be a Godly husband, I learned there is this type of man that the Bible speaks of. He's not in the book of Proverbs, but the rather in the book of Ephesians. He is known as the Ephesians five man. So who is he?

Well, he's not any one man in particular. He's just that type man that most women would find worthy of marrying. So, what made this Ephesians five man such a phenomenal husband? This man loves his wife as Christ loved the church. Now, while that sounds good, let me remind you that Christ *died* for the church. Died! After pondering on this thought, I prayed, "No Thank You Lord, this single life will do." I felt as though the Lord was telling me, "You ain't ready go sit down somewhere" and I couldn't have been happier. "Ain't nobody got time to be out here dying, girl bye." I walked around upset, because women have to submit unto their husbands according to scripture, but men have to die. That's not fair. "I'll submit Lord, and let her die, cause, I'm not dying."

Finally, I caught the revelation of the text. This death was a death unto self. When the man dies "I" no longer exists in the equation and it's now a matter of "we". When the man dies to self, it makes it easier for a woman to submit to his leading because his ego, pride, and selfishness are all put to death. When a woman understands that a man is willing to lay down his life so they can have a life together, she will follow his leading without hesitation. God was so serious about men treating women with love and care that He warns them that He's a protective father to His daughters. The latter part of 1 Peter 3:7 talks about how a husband should treat his wife right so his prayers won't be hindered. In other words, God says He doesn't want to hear you running your mouth to Him, if you're not treating your wife right. I don't know about you but the last person I want upset at me is the Man upstairs. To be that husband material I desire to be is to be ready to lay down my ego, pride and all my

selfish ways for the woman that I love. Dear

God, this challenge is accepted.

Chapter Eleven

Meet Your Requirements

I learned a valuable lesson in that God

will not give you what you're not ready for.

Oh Lord send me the best woman in town,

but are you the best man in town? I may

desire a queen, but only a king is fit for a

queen. As a king, I would rather wait alone

for my queen than to have a peasant

occupy the position reserved for my queen.

In other words, I love my future wife way

too much to sleep with anyone else. It doesn't matter how much muscle I have, if I can't control my sexual drive then I am weak and lack inner strength. John, do you even know who your future wife is? Nope, but whoever she is I want to make her the happiest woman alive. The truth is, no woman wants a man who's been with everybody, doing everything either.

Marriage is ministry and if I don't practice self-control now, I won't automatically be able to fight these urges after marriage. Many men carry the belief that once they get married every other woman will just automatically stop looking good to them. That's not a risk that I'm willing to take. I refuse to be one who entertains every piece of attention that comes my way. I cannot receive what God has for me, if my hand are still full with what the devil gave me. I want to be the type of man that not every woman can get. Yes, I want to be a man with standards. Well John, all this work for a woman who is not your wife yet? Yes. The Bible says, "So Jacob served seven years for Rachel, AND THEY SEEMED ONLY A FEW DAYS TO HIM

BECAUSE OF THE LOVE HE HAD FOR HER" Genesis 29:20.(NKJV)

John, you don't think that you are doing way too much? Not at all. See, I read somewhere that being good towards your woman is a gift to yourself, because the better you treat her, the better she's going to treat you. There is a level of freedom that a wife has based on the level of loyalty her husband extends to her.

Chapter Twelve

Wives Hold the Keys that Unlock God's Favor in a Husband's Life

The LORD God said, "It is not good for the man to be alone. I will make a helper suitable for him." Genesis 2:18(NIV) Now some (like the Apostle Paul) made it very clear that they

John Momplaisir

are gifted in the area of singleness. It is with

great joy and pleasure that I can shout it out

from the mountain top that I am not the

Apostle Paul and I am not gifted in that area.

I know I need a wife. I don't just want a wife, I

know without a shadow of doubt that I NEED

a wife. "He who finds a wife finds what is

good and receives favor from the LORD."

Proverbs 18:22(NIV) It Appears to me that

there is a level of favor that is attached to a

wife. So no matter how high I go in life there

is something about a wife that has the ability

to help take me to the next level. If my future

78

wife has the ability to unlock God's favor in

my life, then it is safe to say that she's one

woman that I can't live without.

John Momplaisir

To My Daughters

Anecia & Heaven Momplaisir

I write this from my heart, with proud tears streaming down my cheeks. While many women will admit that their Dad broke their hearts long before any boy had the chance to, I promise to be the protector of your hearts. As a father, I know that I'll be the point of reference and definition for what a man is to look like. As your father, I open doors for you girls and pull your seats out not because y'all can't do it yourselves, but because I want to model for you what chivalry is to look like. As I write this, I can almost hear the both of you saying, "Daddy, I'm a big girl." And, I know, I know y'all are grown in your heads, but you'll always be my princesses. When I read this to you girls, please don't roll your eyes until I'm finished. I study you little ladies, because I want you to know that a man's job is to always learn what puts a smile on the face of the lady that matters most to him. I treat the both of you with the utmost respect, because I understand that I set the standard on how a man should treat a lady and I'm trusting that as y'all grow older that you will never settle for anything less.

God has used the both of you to be such an inspiration in my life. I know it looks like I'm doing most of the teaching, but I learn so much from the both of you. I committed myself to learning about y'all from the moment ya'll were born. It may be annoying, but I fight to spend so much time with you girls because time to children equals love. You may not understand it now, but my time is more valuable than money. I know, "but Daddy, your time has never bought us any toys, your money did".

As you grow older, you'll realize that I can always make money, but I won't always be able to make up for lost time. No, I can't teach y'all how to be ladies, but I can teach both of you how a lady should be treated. I want y'all to understand that you never have to compete with anyone, ever. I have one Anecia and one Heaven. There can never be another Anecia and there can never be another Heaven. You girls are beautiful, and you're small, but you have very big hearts made of pure gold. I correct y'all because I see so much more and know you can accomplish so much. God entrusted me with a platform to speak into the life of others, but I also know that I am a forerunner called to open doors for the two of you to walk in. The platform is not for me, but for you. I write and read this not because y'all will understand it all, but because it will make sense in its perfect timing. I want to tell my little angels that I love y'all beyond measure and there is absolutely nothing you little ladies can do to change that. Oh, and I better get my hugs after I read this to y'all.

Dear Future Wife

I probably haven't even met you yet or maybe I did, but I feel like I've known you almost all of my life. I'm praying for you, and for us. I can't wait to protect you and inspire you. I can't wait to lead you with love, and listen to you. As your king, I will hold you tight and fight for you. While holding you tight, I will always remind you that you're the only woman in my world. I will put no other woman above you and I will be one with you. I will not just say I love you every night, but I'll aim to prove it every day. I will not only choose you, but I'll keep choosing you under every circumstance and over everyone. I can't wait to look into your eyes and speak to your spirit and say, "I do," but more importantly I can't wait to still be reminding you that "I still do" many years later. I know how rare you are and there isn't another woman worth me losing you. I know that no matter how good I look to others that I'm never fully dressed without you on my arm. The day I meet you all I want is to hear God whisper is "She's the one." I want to go out of my way to make it obvious to you that I want you in

my life. I can't promise perfection, but I
have enough sense not to allow pride and
ego to ever make me lose you. Whoever
you are, I know that you will be the proof
that God answers prayers and gives His
children the desires of their heart. As a
woman, you'll never have to try to prove to
anyone that I love you, that's my job.
Regardless of what life sends our way, we'll
go through it together and get through it
together. My love for you will make you
question if you've ever known love before
and prove to you why your first love wasn't
really your first love. I can't wait to flirt with

you and still be flirting with you years later, even after we've gotten married. Because I have set my heart on you, everyone else who wants me becomes irrelevant. While I know you'll be fashionable and wearing the heck out of a pencil skirt, I can't wait to see you wear my last name with confidence. I know the both of us will get tempted, but I know we'll survive if we can remember that no temptation will be worth losing what we have. I'm committed to proving to you all men aren't the same, because I can't afford to sleep on the one that I've dreamt of for so long. My goal is train myself to be so busy paying attention to you that I don't

have time to entertain any other woman.

While protecting a woman's sexual integrity

is the highest form of respect that a man

can display, after marriage you're going to

get a double portion of a special anointing

on demand (I'll explain that when we meet).

I can't wait to mentally stimulate you with

erotic love notes and cause your rivers of

living waters to flow. I plan on messing your

mind up so badly that you can't even focus

at your place of employment, if you decide

to work. I hope you don't work full time in

ministry and pray for folks all day, cause

they're going to be wondering what kind of sex spirit you imparted on them. I can't wait to meet you. We're going to be the best of friends, confidants, and we're going to be two hearts which beat as one.

I can't wait to grow in love with you, and one day we're going to have a marriage ministry and bring hope back to marriages. I can't wait to inspire others with you, and love you over and over again.

Okay, Bye.